CW01082612

The Little Book of Christian Hymns

David P. Boyd

ISBN-13: 9781074568085

DEDICATION

To all those who struggle, may you find hope.

CONTENTS

Let your heart guide you to the Hymn that's right for you

ACKNOWLEDGMENTS

Thank you to all who helped with this publication.

AMAZING GRACE

Amazing Grace, how sweet the sound,
That saved a wretch like me....
I once was lost but now am found,
Was blind, but now, I see.

T'was Grace that taught...
my heart to fear.
And Grace, my fears relieved.
How precious did that Grace appear...
the hour I first believed.

Through many dangers, toils and snares...
we have already come.
T'was Grace that brought us safe thus far...
and Grace will lead us home.

The Lord has promised good to me...
His word my hope secures.
He will my shield and portion be...
as long as life endures.

When we've been here ten thousand years...
bright shining as the sun.
We've no less days to sing God's praise...
then when we've first begun.

Amazing Grace, how sweet the sound,
That saved a wretch like me....
I once was lost but now am found,
Was blind, but now, I see.

ABIDE WITH ME

Abide with me; fast falls the eventide;
The darkness deepens; Lord with me abide.
When other helpers fail and comforts flee,
Help of the helpless, O abide with me.

Swift to its close ebbs out life's little day;
Earth's joys grow dim; its glories pass away;
Change and decay in all around I see;
O Thou who changest not, abide with me.

Not a brief glance I beg, a passing word;
But as Thou dwell'st with Thy disciples, Lord,
Familiar, condescending, patient, free.
Come not to sojourn, but abide with me.

Come not in terrors, as the King of kings,
But kind and good, with healing in Thy wings,
Tears for all woes, a heart for every plea—
Come, Friend of sinners, and thus bide with me.

Thou on my head in early youth didst smile;
And, though rebellious and perverse meanwhile,
Thou hast not left me, oft as I left Thee,
On to the close, O Lord, abide with me.

I need Thy presence every passing hour.
What but Thy grace can foil the tempter's power?
Who, like Thyself, my guide and stay can be?
Through cloud and sunshine, Lord, abide with me.

I fear no foe, with Thee at hand to bless;
Ills have no weight, and tears no bitterness.
Where is death's sting? Where, grave, thy victory?
I triumph still, if Thou abide with me.

Hold Thou Thy cross before my closing eyes;
Shine through the gloom and point me to the skies.
Heaven's morning breaks, and earth's vain shadows flee;
In life, in death, O Lord, abide with me.

ALL THINGS BRIGHT AND BEAUTIFUL

All things bright and beautiful,
All creatures great and small,
All things wise and wonderful,
The Lord God made them all.

Each little flower that opens,
Each little bird that sings,
He made their glowing colours,
He made their tiny wings.

All things bright and beautiful,
All creatures great and small,
All things wise and wonderful,
The Lord God made them all

The purple-headed mountain,
The river running by,
The sunset and the morning,
That brightens up the sky;

All things bright and beautiful,
All creatures great and small,
All things wise and wonderful,
The Lord God made them all

The cold wind in the winter,
The pleasant summer sun,
The ripe fruits in the garden,
He made them every one;

All things bright and beautiful,
All creatures great and small,
All things wise and wonderful,
The Lord God made them all

The tall trees in the greenwood,
The meadows for our play,
The rushes by the water,
To gather every day;

All things bright and beautiful,
All creatures great and small,
All things wise and wonderful,
The Lord God made them all

He gave us eyes to see them,
And lips that we might tell
How great is God Almighty,
Who has made all things well.

All things bright and beautiful,
All creatures great and small,
All things wise and wonderful,
The Lord God made them all.

BE STILL MY SOUL

Be still, my soul; the Lord is on thy side;
Bear patiently the cross of grief or pain;
Leave to thy God to order and provide;
In every change He faithful will remain.
Be still, my soul; thy best, thy heavenly, Friend
Through thorny ways leads to a joyful end.

Be still, my soul; thy God doth undertake
To guide the future as He has the past.
Thy hope, thy confidence, let nothing shake;
All now mysterious shall be bright at last.
Be still, my soul; the waves and winds still know
His voice who ruled them while He dwelt below.

Be still, my soul, though dearest friends depart
And all is darkened in the vale of tears;
Then shalt thou better know His love, His heart,
Who comes to soothe thy sorrows and thy fears.
Be still, my soul; thy Jesus can repay
From His own fulness all He takes away.

Be still, my soul; the hour is hastening on
When we shall be forever with the Lord,
When disappointment, grief, and fear are gone,
Sorrow forgot, love's purest joys restored.
Be still, my soul; when change and tears are past,
All safe and blessed we shall meet at last.

AVE MARIA

Ave Maria! Ave Maria! maiden mild!
Listen to a maiden's prayer!
Thou canst hear though from the wild,
Thou canst save amid despair.
Safe may we sleep beneath thy care,
Though banish'd, outcast and reviled -
Maiden! hear a maiden's prayer;
Mother, hear a suppliant child!
Ave Maria!

Ave Maria! undefiled!
The flinty couch we now must share
Shall seem this down of eider piled,
If thy protection hover there.
The murky cavern's heavy air
Shall breathe of balm if thou hast smiled;
Then, Maiden! hear a maiden's prayer;
Mother, list a suppliant child!
Ave Maria!

Ave Maria! stainless styled!
Foul demons of the earth and air,
From this their wonted haunt exiled,
Shall flee before thy presence fair.
We bow us to our lot of care,
Beneath thy guidance reconciled;
Hear for a maid a maiden's prayer,
And for a father hear a child!
Ave Maria!

ROCK OF AGES

Rock of Ages, cleft for me,
Let me hide myself in Thee;
Let the water and the blood,
From Thy wounded side which flowed,
Be of sin the double cure;
Save from wrath and make me pure.

Not the labor of my hands
Can fulfill Thy law's demands;
Could my zeal no respite know,
Could my tears forever flow,
All for sin could not atone;
Thou must save, and Thou alone.

Nothing in my hand I bring,
Simply to the cross I cling;
Naked, come to Thee for dress;
Helpless look to Thee for grace;
Foul, I to the fountain fly;
Wash me, Savior, or I die.

While I draw this fleeting breath,
When mine eyes shall close in death,
When I soar to worlds unknown,
See Thee on Thy judgment throne,
Rock of Ages, cleft for me,
Let me hide myself in Thee

THE LORD IS MY SHEPARD

The Lord's my shepherd, I'll not want;
He makes me down to lie
In pastures green; he leadeth me
The quiet waters by.

My soul he doth restore again,
And me to walk doth make
Within the paths of righteousness,
E'en for his own name's sake.

Yea, though I walk in death's dark vale,
Yet will I fear no ill:
For thou art with me, and thy rod
And staff me comfort still.

My table thou hast furnished
In presence of my foes;
My head thou dost with oil anoint
And my cup overflows.

Goodness and mercy all my life
Shall surely follow me;
And in God's house for evermore
My dwelling-place shall be.

ONWARD CHRISTIAN SOLIDERS

Onward, Christian soldiers, marching as to war,
With the cross of Jesus going on before.
Christ, the royal Master, leads against the foe;
Forward into battle see His banners go!

Refrain

Onward, Christian soldiers, marching as to war,
With the cross of Jesus going on before.

At the sign of triumph Satan's host doth flee;
On then, Christian soldiers, on to victory!
Hell's foundations quiver at the shout of praise;
Brothers lift your voices, loud your anthems raise.

Refrain

Like a mighty army moves the church of God;
Brothers, we are treading where the saints have trod.
We are not divided, all one body we,
One in hope and doctrine, one in charity.

Refrain

What the saints established that I hold for true.
What the saints believèd, that I believe too.
Long as earth endureth, men the faith will hold,
Kingdoms, nations, empires, in destruction rolled.

Refrain

Crowns and thrones may perish, kingdoms rise and wane,
But the church of Jesus constant will remain.
Gates of hell can never gainst that church prevail;
We have Christ's own promise, and that cannot fail.

Refrain

Onward then, ye people, join our happy throng,
Blend with ours your voices in the triumph song.
Glory, laud and honor unto Christ the King,
This through countless ages men and angels sing.

Refrain

PEACE PERFECT PEACE

Peace, perfect peace, in this dark world of sin?
The blood of Jesus whispers peace within.

Peace, perfect peace, by thronging duties pressed?
To do the will of Jesus, this is rest.

Peace, perfect peace, with sorrow surging round?
In Jesus's presence nought but calm is found.

Peace, perfect peace, with loved ones far away?
In Jesus's keeping we are safe, and they.

Peace, perfect peace, our future all unknown?
Jesus we know, and He is on the throne.

Peace, perfect peace, death shadowing us and ours?
Jesus has vanquished death and all its powers

It is enough: earth's struggles soon shall cease,
and Jesus call us to heaven's perfect peace

ETERNITY

Hear the passing bells of time,
Ring the dirge of moments dead,
Golden hours whose joys are fled—
Still those bells of time we hear,
Tolling, tolling: Hark! the word:

Refrain

Eternity!
Eternity!
Eternity!

In the rosy morning fair,
In the sultry noonday glare,
In the dewy evening bright,
In the silent hush of night—
Still those bells of time we hear,
Tolling, tolling, loud and clear:

Refrain

When with breaking heart we bend,
O'er a tried and faithful friend,
When the parting hour draws nigh,
And we catch the last "goodbye"—
Still those bells of time we hear,
Tolling, tolling, loud and clear:

Refrain

Precious word! if safe we stand
On the Christian's borderland
Trusting Him, Whose loving smile
Lights and cheers us all the while—
Bells of time with joy we hear,
Tolling, tolling, sweet and clear:

Refrain

ASLEEP IN JESUS

Asleep in Jesus! Blessed sleep,
From which none ever wakes to weep;
A calm and undisturbed repose,
Unbroken by the last of foes.

Asleep in Jesus! Oh, how sweet,
To be for such a slumber meet,
With holy confidence to sing
That death has lost his venomed sting!

Asleep in Jesus! Peaceful rest,
Whose waking is supremely blessed;
No fear, no woe, shall dim that hour
That manifests the Savior's power.

Asleep in Jesus! Oh, for me
May such a blessèd refuge be!
Securely shall my ashes lie
And wait the summons from on high.

Asleep in Jesus! time nor space
Debars this precious "hiding place";
On Indian plains or Lapland snows
Believers find the same respose.

Asleep in Jesus! Far from thee
Thy kindred and their graves may be;
But there is still a blessèd sleep,
From which none ever wakes to weep.

BE THOU MY VISION HYMN

Be Thou my Vision, O Lord of my heart;
Naught be all else to me, save that Thou art
Thou my best Thought, by day or by night,
Waking or sleeping, Thy presence my light.

Be Thou my Wisdom, and Thou my true Word;
I ever with Thee and Thou with me, Lord;
Thou my great Father, I Thy true son;
Thou in me dwelling, and I with Thee one.

Be Thou my battle Shield, Sword for the fight;
Be Thou my Dignity, Thou my Delight;
Thou my soul's Shelter, Thou my high Tower:
Raise Thou me heavenward, O Power of my power.

Riches I heed not, nor man's empty praise,
Thou mine Inheritance, now and always:
Thou and Thou only, first in my heart,
High King of Heaven, my Treasure Thou art.

High King of Heaven, my victory won,
May I reach Heaven's joys, O bright Heaven's Sun!
Heart of my own heart, whatever befall,
Still be my Vision, O Ruler of all.

IT IS WELL WITH MY SOUL HYMN

When peace, like a river, attendeth my way,
When sorrows like sea billows roll;
Whatever my lot, Thou has taught me to say,
It is well, it is well, with my soul.

Refrain

It is well, with my soul,
It is well, with my soul,
It is well, it is well, with my soul.

Though Satan should buffet, though trials should come,
Let this blest assurance control,
That Christ has regarded my helpless estate,
And hath shed His own blood for my soul.

Refrain

My sin, oh, the bliss of this glorious thought!
My sin, not in part but the whole,
Is nailed to the cross, and I bear it no more,
Praise the Lord, praise the Lord, O my soul!

Refrain

For me, be it Christ, be it Christ hence to live:
If Jordan above me shall roll,
No pang shall be mine, for in death as in life
Thou wilt whisper Thy peace to my soul.

Refrain

But, Lord, 'tis for Thee, for Thy coming we wait,
The sky, not the grave, is our goal;
Oh trump of the angel! Oh voice of the Lord!
Blessed hope, blessed rest of my soul!

Refrain

And Lord, haste the day when my faith shall be sight,
The clouds be rolled back as a scroll;
The trump shall resound, and the Lord shall descend,
Even so, it is well with my soul.

Refrain

IN THE GARDEN HYMN

I come to the garden alone
While the dew is still on the roses
And the voice I hear falling on my ear
The Son of God discloses.

Refrain

And He walks with me, and He talks with me,
And He tells me I am His own;
And the joy we share as we tarry there,
None other has ever known.

He speaks, and the sound of His voice,
Is so sweet the birds hush their singing,
And the melody that He gave to me
Within my heart is ringing.

Refrain

I'd stay in the garden with Him
Though the night around me be falling,
But He bids me go; through the voice of woe
His voice to me is calling.

Refrain

THIS LITTLE LIGHT OF MINE HYMN

This little light of mine, I'm gonna let it shine.
This little light of mine, I'm gonna let it shine, let it shine, let it shine, let it
shine.

Won't let Satan blow it out.
I'm gonna let it shine.
Won't let Satan blow it out.
I'm gonna let it shine, let it shine, let it shine, let it shine.

Let it shine til Jesus comes.
I'm gonna let it shine.
Let it shine til Jesus comes.
I'm gonna let it shine, let it shine, let it shine, let it shine.

Hide it under a bushel - NO!
I'm gonna let it shine.
Hide it under a bushel - NO!
I'm gonna let it shine, Let it shine, let it shine, let it shine.

Let it shine over the whole wide world,
I'm gonna let it shine.
Let it shine over the whole wide world,
I'm gonna let it shine, let it shine, let it shine, let it shine.

JUST A CLOSER WALK WITH THEE HYMN

I am weak, but Thou art strong;
Jesus, keep me from all wrong;
I'll be satisfied as long
As I walk, let me walk close to Thee.

Refrain

Just a closer walk with Thee,
Grant it, Jesus, is my plea,
Daily walking close to Thee,
Let it be, dear Lord, let it be.

Through this world of toil and snares,
If I falter, Lord, who cares?
Who with me my burden shares?
None but Thee, dear Lord, none but Thee.

Refrain

When my feeble life is o'er,
Time for me will be no more;
Guide me gently, safely o'er
To Thy kingdom shore, to Thy shore.

Refrain

NEARER MY GOD TO THEE HYMN

Nearer, my God, to Thee, nearer to Thee!
E'en though it be a cross that raiseth me,
Still all my song shall be, nearer, my God, to Thee.

Refrain

Nearer, my God, to Thee,
Nearer to Thee!

Though like the wanderer, the sun gone down,
Darkness be over me, my rest a stone.
Yet in my dreams I'd be nearer, my God to Thee.

Refrain

There let the way appear, steps unto Heav'n;
All that Thou sendest me, in mercy given;
Angels to beckon me nearer, my God, to Thee.

Refrain

Then, with my waking thoughts bright with Thy praise,
Out of my stony griefs Bethel I'll raise;
So by my woes to be nearer, my God, to Thee.

Refrain

Or, if on joyful wing cleaving the sky,
Sun, moon, and stars forgot, upward I'll fly,
Still all my song shall be, nearer, my God, to Thee.

Refrain

There in my Father's home, safe and at rest,
There in my Saviour's love, perfectly blest;
Age after age to be, nearer my God to Thee.

Refrain

BLESSED ASSURANCE HYMN

Blessed assurance, Jesus is mine!
O what a foretaste of glory divine!
Heir of salvation, purchase of God,
Born of His Spirit, washed in His blood.

Refrain

This is my story, this is my song,
Praising my Saviour, all the day long;
This is my story, this is my song,
Praising my Saviour, all the day long.

Perfect submission, perfect delight,
Visions of rapture now burst on my sight;
Angels descending bring from above
Echoes of mercy, whispers of love.

Refrain

Perfect submission, all is at rest
I in my Saviour am happy and blest,
Watching and waiting, looking above,
Filled with His goodness, lost in His love.

Refrain

PSALM 23

The Lord's my shepherd, I'll not want;
He makes me down to lie
In pastures green; he leadeth me
The quiet waters by.

My soul he doth restore again,
And me to walk doth make
Within the paths of righteousness,
Even for his own name's sake.

Yea, though I walk in death's dark vale,
Yet will I fear no ill:
For thou art with me, and thy rod
And staff me comfort still.

My table thou hast furnished
In presence of my foes;
My head thou dost with oil anoint
And my cup overflows.

Goodness and mercy all my life
Shall surely follow me;
And in God's house for evermore
My dwelling-place shall be.

THE OLD RUGGED CROSS

On a hill far away stood an old rugged cross,
The emblem of suffering and shame;
And I love that old cross where the dearest and best
For a world of lost sinners was slain.

Refrain

So I'll cherish the old rugged cross,
Till my trophies at last I lay down;
I will cling to the old rugged cross,
And exchange it some day for a crown.

O that old rugged cross, so despised by the world,
Has a wondrous attraction for me;
For the dear Lamb of God left His glory above
To bear it to dark Calvary.

Refrain

In that old rugged cross, stained with blood so divine,
A wondrous beauty I see,
For 'twas on that old cross Jesus suffered and died,
To pardon and sanctify me.

Refrain

To the old rugged cross I will ever be true;
Its shame and reproach gladly bear;
Then He'll call me some day to my home far away,
Where His glory forever I'll share.

HE WHO WOULD VALIANT BE HYMN

He who would valiant be against all disaster,
Let him in constancy follow the Master.
There's no discouragement shall make him once relent
His first avowed intent to be a pilgrim.

Who so beset him round with dismal stories
Do but themselves confound - his strength the more is.
No foes shall stay his might; though he with giants fight,
He will make good his right to be a pilgrim.

Since, Lord, Thou dost defend us with Thy Spirit,
We know we at the end, shall life inherit.
Then fancies flee away! I'll fear not what men say,
I'll labor night and day to be a pilgrim.

WE PLOUGH THE FIELDS AND SCATTER HYMN

We plough the fields and scatter
The good seed on the land,
But it is fed and watered
By God's almighty hand:
He sends the snow in winter,
The warmth to swell the grain,
The breezes and the sunshine,
And soft, refreshing rain.

Refrain:
All good gifts around us
Are sent from heaven above;
Then thank the Lord,
O thank the Lord,
For all his love.

He only is the maker
Of all things near and far;
He paints the wayside flower,
He lights the evening star;
The winds and waves obey him,
By him the birds are fed;
Much more to us, his children,
He gives our daily bread.

We thank thee then, O Father,
For all things bright and good,
The seed time and the harvest,
Our life, our health, our food.
Accept the gifts we offer
For all thy love imparts,
And what thou most desires
Our humble, thankful hearts.

Refrain

ETERNAL FATHER STRONG TO SAVE HYMN

Eternal Father, strong to save,
Whose arm hath bound the restless wave,
Who biddest the mighty ocean deep
Its own appointed limits keep;
Oh, hear us when we cry to Thee,
For those in peril on the sea!

O Christ! Whose voice the waters heard
And hushed their raging at Thy Word,
Who walked on the foaming deep,
And calm amidst its rage didst sleep;
Oh, hear us when we cry to Thee,
For those in peril on the sea!

Most Holy Spirit! Who didst brood
Upon the chaos dark and rude,
And bid its angry tumult cease,
And give, for wild confusion, peace;
Oh, hear us when we cry to Thee,
For those in peril on the sea!

O Trinity of love and power!
Our family shield in danger's hour;
From rock and tempest, fire and foe,
Protect us wheresoever we go;
Thus evermore shall rise to Thee
Glad hymns of praise from land and sea.

JESUS LOVER OF MY SOUL HYMN

Jesus, lover of my soul, let me to Thy bosom fly,
While the nearer waters roll, while the tempest still is high.
Hide me, O my Saviour, hide, till the storm of life is past;
Safe into the haven guide; O receive my soul at last.

Other refuge have I none, hangs my helpless soul on Thee;
Leave, ah! leave me not alone, still support and comfort me.
All my trust on Thee is stayed, all my help from Thee I bring;
Cover my defenceless head with the shadow of Thy wing.

Wilt Thou not regard my call? Wilt Thou not accept my prayer?
Lo! I sink, I faint, I fall - Lo! on Thee I cast my care;
Reach me out Thy gracious hand! While I of Thy strength receive,
Hoping against hope I stand, dying, and behold, I live.

Thou, O Christ, art all I want, more than all in Thee I find;
Raise the fallen, cheer the faint, heal the sick, and lead the blind.
Just and holy is Thy Name, I am all unrighteousness;
False and full of sin I am; Thou art full of truth and grace.

Plenteous grace with Thee is found, grace to cover all my sin;
Let the healing streams abound; make and keep me pure within.
Thou of life the fountain art, freely let me take of Thee;
Spring Thou up within my heart; rise to all eternity.

I COME TO THE GARDEN ALONE

I come to the garden alone
While the dew is still on the roses
And the voice I hear falling on my ear
The Son of God discloses.

Refrain

And He walks with me, and He talks with me,
And He tells me I am His own;
And the joy we share as we tarry there,
None other has ever known.

He speaks, and the sound of His voice,
Is so sweet the birds hush their singing,
And the melody that He gave to me
Within my heart is ringing.

Refrain

I'd stay in the garden with Him
Though the night around me be falling,
But He bids me go; through the voice of woe
His voice to me is calling.

Refrain

BREATH OF GOD

Breathe on me, breath of God,
Fill me with life anew,
That I may love what Thou dost love,
And do what Thou wouldst do.

Breathe on me, breath of God,
Until my heart is pure,
Until with Thee I will one will,
To do and to endure.

Breathe on me, breath of God,
Blend all my soul with Thine,
Until this earthly part of me
Glows with Thy fire divine.

Breathe on me, breath of God,
So shall I never die,
But live with Thee the perfect life
Of Thine eternity.

LIFT HIGH THE CROSS

Lift high the cross, the love of Christ proclaim,
Till all the world adore His sacred Name.

Led on their way by this triumphant sign,
The hosts of God in conquering ranks combine.

Refrain

Each newborn servant of the Crucified
Bears on the brow the seal of Him Who died.

Refrain

O Lord, once lifted on the glorious tree,
As Thou hast promised, draw the world to Thee.

Refrain

So shall our song of triumph ever be:
Praise to the Crucified for victory.

Refrain

THE HOLY CITY

Last night I lay a-sleeping
There came a dream so fair,
I stood in old Jerusalem
Beside the temple there.
I heard the children singing,
And ever as they sang,
Me thought the voice of angels
From heaven in answer rang.

Jerusalem! Jerusalem!
Lift up your gates and sing,
Hosanna in the highest!
Hosanna to your King!

And then me thought my dream was changed,
The streets no longer rang,
Hushed were the glad Hosannas
The little children sang.
The sun grew dark with mystery,
The morn was cold and chill,
As the shadow of a cross arose
Upon a lonely hill.

Jerusalem! Jerusalem!
Hark! How the angels sing,
Hosanna in the highest!
Hosanna to your King!

And once again the scene was changed;
New earth there seemed to be;
I saw the Holy City
Beside the tideless sea;
The light of God was on its streets,
The gates were open wide,
And all who would might enter,
And no one was denied.

No need of moon or stars by night,
Or sun to shine by day;
It was the new Jerusalem
That would not pass away.

Jerusalem! Jerusalem!
Sing for the night is o'er!
Hosanna in the highest!
Hosanna for evermore!

FIGHT THE GOOD FIGHT

Fight the good fight with all thy might;
Christ is thy Strength, and Christ thy Right;
Lay hold on life, and it shall be
Thy joy and crown eternally.

Run the straight race through God's good grace,
Lift up thine eyes, and seek His face;
Life with its way before us lies,
Christ is the Path, and Christ the Prize.

Cast care aside, upon thy Guide,
Lean, and His mercy will provide;
Lean, and the trusting soul shall prove
Christ is its Life, and Christ its Love.

Faint not nor fear, His arms are near,
He changeth not, and thou art dear.
Only believe, and thou shalt see
That Christ is all in all to thee.

JESUS LOVES ME THIS I KNOW

Jesus loves me! This I know,
For the Bible tells me so.
Little ones to Him belong;
They are weak, but He is strong.

Refrain

Yes, Jesus loves me!
Yes, Jesus loves me!
Yes, Jesus loves me!
The Bible tells me so.

Jesus loves me! This I know,
As He loved so long ago,
Taking children on His knee,
Saying, "Let them come to Me."

Refrain

Jesus loves me still today,
Walking with me on my way,
Wanting as a friend to give
Light and love to all who live.

Refrain

Jesus loves me! He who died
Heaven's gate to open wide;
He will wash away my sin,
Let His little child come in.

Refrain

Jesus loves me! He will stay
Close beside me all the way;

Thou hast bled and died for me,
I will henceforth live for Thee.

AT THE CROSS

Mourner, wheresoever thou art,
  At the cross there's room!
Tell the burden of thy heart,
  At the cross there's room!
Tell it in thy Saviour's ear,
Cast away thine every fear,
Only speak, and He will hear;
  At the cross there's room!

Haste thee, wand'rer, tarry not,
  At the cross there's room!
Seek that consecrated spot;
  At the cross there's room!
Heavy laden, sore oppressed,
Love can soothe thy troubled breast;
In the Saviour find thy rest;
  At the cross there's room!

Thoughtless sinner, come today;
  At the cross there's room!
Hark! the Bride and Spirit say,
  At the cross there's room!
Now a living fountain see,
Opened there for you and me,
Rich and poor, for bond and free,
  At the cross there's room!

Blessed thought! For every one
  At the cross there's room!
Love's atoning work is done;
  At the cross there's room!
Streams of boundless mercy flow,

Free to all who thither go;
Oh, that all the world might know
At the cross there's room!

FOR THE BEAUTY OF THE EARTH

For the beauty of the earth,
For the beauty of the skies,
For the love which from our birth
Over and around us lies,
Lord of all, to thee we raise
This our grateful hymn of praise.

For the beauty of each hour
Of the day and of the night,
Hill and vale, and tree and flower,
Sun and moon and stars of light,
Lord of all, to thee we raise
This our grateful hymn of praise.

For the joy of human love,
Brother, sister, parent, child,
Friends on earth, and friends above,
Pleasures pure and undefiled,
Lord of all, to thee we raise
This our grateful hymn of praise.

For each perfect gift of thine,
To our race so freely given,
Graces human and divine,
Flowers of earth and buds of heaven,
Lord of all, to thee we raise
This our grateful hymn of praise.

For thy Church which evermore
Lifteth holy hands above,
Offering up on every shore
Her pure sacrifice of love,

Lord of all, to thee we raise
This our grateful hymn of praise.

JESUS CHRIST IS RISEN TODAY

Christ, the Lord, is risen today, Alleluia!
Sons of men and angels say, Alleluia!
Raise your joys and triumphs high, Alleluia!
Sing, ye heavens, and earth, reply, Alleluia!

Love's redeeming work is done, Alleluia!
Fought the fight, the battle won, Alleluia!
Lo! the Sun's eclipse is over, Alleluia!
Lo! He sets in blood no more, Alleluia!

Vain the stone, the watch, the seal, Alleluia!
Christ hath burst the gates of hell, Alleluia!
Death in vain forbids His rise, Alleluia!
Christ hath opened paradise, Alleluia!

Lives again our glorious King, Alleluia!
Where, O death, is now thy sting? Alleluia!
Once He died our souls to save, Alleluia!
Where thy victory, O grave? Alleluia!

Soar we now where Christ hath led, Alleluia!
Following our exalted Head, Alleluia!
Made like Him, like Him we rise, Alleluia!
Ours the cross, the grave, the skies, Alleluia!

Hail, the Lord of earth and heaven, Alleluia!
Praise to Thee by both be given, Alleluia!
Thee we greet triumphant now, Alleluia!
Hail, the resurrection day, Alleluia!

King of glory, Soul of bliss, Alleluia!
Everlasting life is this, Alleluia!
Thee to know, Thy power to prove, Alleluia!

Thus to sing and thus to love, Alleluia!

Hymns of praise then let us sing, Alleluia!
Unto Christ, our heavenly King, Alleluia!

Who endured the cross and grave, Alleluia!
Sinners to redeem and save. Alleluia!

But the pains that He endured, Alleluia!
Our salvation have procured, Alleluia!
Now above the sky He's King, Alleluia!
Where the angels ever sing. Alleluia!

Jesus Christ is risen today, Alleluia!
Our triumphant holy day, Alleluia!
Who did once upon the cross, Alleluia!
Suffer to redeem our loss. Alleluia!

SHALL WE GATHER AT THE RIVER

Shall we gather at the river,
Where bright angel feet have trod,
With its crystal tide forever
Flowing by the throne of God?

Refrain

Yes, we'll gather at the river,
The beautiful, the beautiful river;
Gather with the saints at the river
That flows by the throne of God.

On the margin of the river,
Washing up its silver spray,
We will talk and worship ever,
All the happy golden day.

Refrain

Ere we reach the shining river,
Lay we every burden down;
Grace our spirits will deliver,
And provide a robe and crown.

Refrain

At the smiling of the river,
Mirror of the Saviour's face,
Saints, whom death will never sever,
Lift their songs of saving grace.

Refrain

Soon we'll reach the silver river,
Soon our pilgrimage will cease;
Soon our happy hearts will quiver
With the melody of peace.

ALL HAIL THE POWER OF JESUS NAME

All hail the power of Jesus' Name! Let angels prostrate fall;
Bring forth the royal diadem, and crown Him Lord of all.
Bring forth the royal diadem, and crown Him Lord of all.

Let highborn seraphs tune the lyre, and as they tune it, fall
Before His face Who tunes their choir, and crown Him Lord of all.
Before His face Who tunes their choir, and crown Him Lord of all.

Crown Him, ye morning stars of light, Who fixed this floating ball;
Now hail the strength of Israel's might, and crown Him Lord of all.
Now hail the strength of Israel's might, and crown Him Lord of all.

Crown Him, ye martyrs of your God, who from His altar call;
Extol the Stem of Jesse's Rod, and crown Him Lord of all.
Extol the Stem of Jesse's Rod, and crown Him Lord of all.

Ye seed of Israel's chosen race, ye ransomed from the fall,
Hail Him Who saves you by His grace, and crown Him Lord of all.
Hail Him Who saves you by His grace, and crown Him Lord of all.

Hail Him, ye heirs of David's line, Whom David Lord did call,
The God incarnate, Man divine, and crown Him Lord of all,
The God incarnate, Man divine, and crown Him Lord of all.

Sinners, whose love can ne'er forget the wormwood and the gall,
Go spread your trophies at His feet, and crown Him Lord of all.
Go spread your trophies at His feet, and crown Him Lord of all.

Let every tribe and every tongue before Him prostrate fall
And shout in universal song the crowned Lord of all.
And shout in universal song the crowned Lord of all.

FAIREST LORD JESUS HYMN

Fairest Lord Jesus, Ruler of all nature,
O Thou of God and man the Son,
Thee will I cherish, Thee will I honor,
Thou, my soul's glory, joy and crown.

Fair are the meadows, fairer still the woodlands,
Robed in the blooming garb of spring;
Jesus is fairer, Jesus is purer,
Who makes the woeful heart to sing.

Fair is the sunshine,
Fairer still the moonlight,
And all the twinkling starry host;
Jesus shines brighter, Jesus shines purer
Than all the angels heaven can boast.

All fairest beauty, heavenly and earthly,
Wondrously, Jesus, is found in Thee;
None can be nearer, fairer or dearer,
Than Thou, my Savior, art to me.

Beautiful Savior! Lord of all the nations!
Son of God and Son of Man!
Glory and honor, praise, adoration,
Now and forever more be Thine.

CROWN HIM WITH MANY CROWNS

Crown Him with many crowns, the Lamb upon His throne.
Hark! How the heavenly anthem drowns all music but its own.
Awake, my soul, and sing of Him who died for thee,
And hail Him as thy matchless King through all eternity.

Crown Him the virgin's Son, the God incarnate born,
Whose arm those crimson trophies won which now His brow adorn;
Fruit of the mystic rose, as of that rose the stem;
The root whence mercy ever flows, the Babe of Bethlehem.

Crown Him the Son of God, before the worlds began,
And ye who tread where He hath trod, crown Him the Son of Man;
Who every grief hath known that wrings the human breast,
And takes and bears them for His own, that all in Him may rest.

Crown Him the Lord of life, who triumphed over the grave,
And rose victorious in the strife for those He came to save.
His glories now we sing, Who died, and rose on high,
Who died eternal life to bring, and lives that death may die.

Crown Him the Lord of peace, Whose power a scepter sways
From pole to pole, that wars may cease, and all be prayer and praise.
His reign shall know no end, and round His pierced feet
Fair flowers of paradise extend their fragrance ever sweet.

Crown Him the Lord of love, behold His hands and side,
Those wounds, yet visible above, in beauty glorified.
No angel in the sky can fully bear that sight,
But downward bends his burning eye at mysteries so bright.

Crown Him the Lord of Heaven, enthroned in worlds above,
Crown Him the King to Whom is given the wondrous name of Love.

Crown Him with many crowns, as thrones before Him fall;
Crown Him, ye kings, with many crowns, for He is King of all.

Crown Him the Lord of lords, who over all doth reign,
Who once on earth, the incarnate Word, for ransomed sinners slain,
Now lives in realms of light, where saints with angels sing
Their songs before Him day and night, their God, Redeemer, King.

Crown Him the Lord of years, the Potentate of time,
Creator of the rolling spheres, ineffably sublime.
All hail, Redeemer, hail! For Thou has died for me;
Thy praise and glory shall not fail throughout eternity.

THE KING OF LOVE MY SHEPHERD

The king of love my shepherd is,
Whose goodness faileth never;
I nothing lack if I am his
And he is mine for ever.

Where streams of living water flow
My ransomed soul he leadeth,
And where the verdant pastures grow
With food celestial feedeth.

Perverse and foolish oft I strayed,
But yet in love he sought me,
And on his shoulder gently laid,
And home rejoicing brought me.

In death's dark vale I fear no ill
With thee, dear Lord, beside me;
Thy rod and staff my comfort still,
Thy cross before to guide me.

Thou spread'st a table in my sight;
Thy unction grace bestoweth;
And O what transport of delight
From thy pure chalice floweth!

And so through all the length of days
Thy goodness faileth never:
Good shepherd, may I sing thy praise
Within thy house for ever.

GIVE ME JOY IN MY HEART

Give me joy in my heart, keep me praising,
Give me joy in my heart, I pray;
Give me joy in my heart, keep me praising,
Keep me praising till the break of day:

Sing hosanna, sing hosanna,
Sing hosanna to the King of kings.
Sing hosanna, sing hosanna,
Sing hosanna to the King.

Give me peace in my heart, keep me loving,
Give me peace in my heart, I pray;
Give me peace in my heart, keep me loving,
Keep me loving till the break of day:

Sing hosanna, sing hosanna,
Sing hosanna to the King of kings.
Sing hosanna, sing hosanna,
Sing hosanna to the King.

Give me love in my heart, keep me serving,
Give me love in my heart, I pray;
Give me love in my heart, keep me serving,
Keep me serving till the break of day:

Sing hosanna, sing hosanna,
Sing hosanna to the King of kings.
Sing hosanna, sing hosanna,
Sing hosanna to the King

FURTHER BIBLICAL READING

For Bishops, Pastors and Preachers: 1 Tim. 3:2-4 Titus 1: 6

What Hearers owe their Pastors: 1 Cor. 9:14 Gal. 6: 6 1 Tim. 5:17-18 Heb. 13:17

For Earthly Authorities
Rom. 13:1-4

For those Under Authority Matt. 22:21 Rom. 13:5-7 1 Tim. 2:1-3 Titus 3:1 1 Peter 2:13-14

For Husbands 1 Peter 3:7 Col. 3:19

For Wives Eph. 5:22 1 Peter 3:5-6

For Parents
Eph. 6:4

For Children
Eph. 6:1-3

For Servants, Maids, Hired Hands and Workers
Eph. 6: 5-7
Col. 3:22

For the Man and Woman of the House
Eph. 6:9
Col. 4:1

For Young People in General 1 Pet. 5:5-6

For Widows 1 Tim. 5:5-6

For Everyone in General Rom. 13:8-10 1 Tim. 2:1-2

ABOUT THE EDITOR

David P. Boyd is a writer, editor and scholar based in Europe.